Harmonizing Imperfections

Finding Balance and Respect in Relationships

Copyright Notice

© 2024 David K. Humble. All rights reserved. No part of this publication may be reproduced, distributed, or transmitted in any form or by any means, including photocopying, recording, or other electronic or mechanical methods, without the express written permission of the copyright holder, except for brief quotations used in critical reviews and certain other non-commercial uses as allowed by applicable copyright law.

Disclaimer

The information provided in this book, "Harmonizing Imperfections: Finding Balance and Respect in Relationships," is intended for general informational purposes only. While every effort has been made to ensure the accuracy and completeness of the information presented, the author and publisher assume no responsibility for errors or omissions, or for any results obtained from the use of the information contained in this book. Readers are encouraged to exercise their own judgment and seek professional advice if needed.

Contents

Introduction 4

Relationships 8

Unveiling Imperfections 32

Boundary in Relationship 40

Acknowledging Fallout 66

Lesson in Accountability 73

The Limits of Manipulation 82

Wisdom in Navigating Relationships 99

Balancing Power and Respect 120

Strategies for Success 135

Embracing Realistic Expectations 160

Finding Harmony in Imperfection 174

Conclusion 183

Introduction

In the web of human connection, relationships weave the intricate threads of our lives, forming the vibrant patterns of our experiences.

Yet, within this rich fabric, imperfections often emerge, like delicate knots and uneven stitches, shaping the texture of our interactions. These imperfections, far from detracting from the beauty of our relationships, offer profound opportunities for growth, understanding, and harmony.

In "Harmonizing Imperfections: Finding Balance and Respect in Relationships," we embark on a journey of exploration into the nuanced dynamics of human connection.

Through the lens of vulnerability and introspection, we navigate the complexities of relationships, delving into essential themes that define our relational landscapes.

Central to our exploration is the unveiling of imperfections—the recognition and acceptance of our own and others' inherent flaws. Within this process lies the cornerstone of authentic connection, where transparency and empathy forge bonds of intimacy and trust.

As we journey further, we encounter the pivotal concept of boundaries in relationships—a delicate dance of self-respect and mutual understanding that delineates the contours of healthy interaction.

Acknowledging fallout becomes a vital aspect of our relational journey, as we confront the aftermath of conflict and misunderstanding with grace and accountability. Through this lens, we glean invaluable lessons in responsibility and forgiveness, nurturing the seeds of resilience and growth within ourselves and our connections.

The exploration extends to the interplay of power and respect, where the limits of manipulation are laid bare, and the wisdom in navigating relationships with integrity and empathy is illuminated. Strategies for success emerge from this crucible of understanding, offering practical tools and insights for fostering thriving connections rooted in authenticity and mutual empowerment.

Yet, amidst these discussions, we embrace the wisdom of embracing realistic expectations—the recognition that perfection is not the goal, but rather the pursuit of harmony amidst imperfection. Through this lens, we uncover the beauty of finding balance and respect in relationships, where every flaw and fracture contributes to the rich mosaic of our shared human experience.

As we embark on this transformative journey, may we find inspiration and guidance in the pages that follow, illuminating the path towards deeper connection, empathy, and harmony amidst the beautiful imperfections of our relationships.

Chapter 1

Relationships

Human relationships refer to the connections, interactions, and bonds that individuals form with one another. These relationships can encompass various aspects of human interaction, including emotional, social, familial, romantic, and professional connections.

At the core of human relationships are elements such as trust, communication, empathy, and mutual understanding.

Human relationships play a vital role in shaping individuals' lives and experiences. They provide support, companionship, and a sense of belonging, contributing to overall well-being and mental health.

Whether it's the bond between family members, the closeness shared between friends, the intimacy of romantic partnerships, or the collaboration and teamwork within professional networks, relationships are fundamental to human existence.

Different types of relationships serve different purposes and fulfill various needs. Family relationships offer love, care, and guidance, while friendships provide companionship, shared experiences, and emotional support. Romantic relationships involve intimacy, passion, and commitment, while professional relationships facilitate collaboration, networking, and career advancement.

Healthy human relationships are characterized by mutual respect, honesty, reciprocity, and open communication. They involve both giving and receiving support, understanding each other's needs, and working together to overcome challenges.

However, relationships can also face difficulties, conflicts, and tensions, which require effort, compromise, and sometimes professional intervention to resolve.

Overall, human relationships are dynamic and multifaceted, enriching our lives with connection, meaning, and fulfillment. They shape our identity, influence our choices and behaviors, and contribute significantly to our happiness and sense of fulfillment.

Types of Relationships

Relationships come in various forms, each with its own dynamics, expectations, and levels of intimacy. Here's an overview of some common types:

1 **Romantic Relationships:**

Characteristics: Emotional and physical intimacy, love, affection, commitment, mutual understanding, shared goals and values, and sexual attraction.

Key Elements: Trust, communication, compromise, support, and respect.

2 **Friendships:**

Characteristics: Mutual affection, trust, loyalty, shared interests, companionship, and emotional support.

Key Elements: Reciprocity, empathy, honesty, acceptance, and the ability to have fun together.

3 **Family Relationships:**

Characteristics: Blood ties or legal connections, unconditional love, shared history, loyalty, and support.

Key Elements: Respect, communication, boundaries, forgiveness, and a sense of belonging.

4 **Professional Relationships:**

Characteristics: Based on work or professional context, mutual respect, collaboration, and shared goals.

Key Elements: Clear communication, professionalism, trust, reliability, and networking.

5 **Casual Relationships:**

Characteristics: Non-committed, primarily focused on enjoyment or convenience, minimal emotional investment.

Key Elements: Informality, spontaneity, mutual consent, and clear boundaries.

6 Online Relationships:

Characteristics: Formed and maintained primarily through digital means, based on shared interests or interactions online.

Key Elements: Communication skills, authenticity, trust, and understanding of online etiquette.

7 Platonic Relationships:

Characteristics: Non-sexual connections, emotional intimacy, camaraderie, and mutual respect.

Key Elements: Boundaries, communication, trust, and the ability to share thoughts and feelings without romantic involvement.

8 **Long-Distance Relationships:**

Characteristics: Partners living far apart, requiring effort to maintain communication and connection.

Key Elements: Trust, communication skills, commitment, and finding ways to bridge the physical distance.

Why do we Keep Relationships

Humans maintain relationships for a multitude of reasons, all of which stem from our inherent social nature and psychological needs. Here are some key reasons why humans engage in relationships:

1 **Emotional Support:** Relationships, whether they be romantic, familial, or friendships, provide emotional support. Having someone to confide in during times of

distress or joy can significantly impact one's mental well-being.

2 **Sense of Belonging:** Relationships give us a sense of belonging and identity. Being part of a community or having close connections reaffirms our place in the world and strengthens our social bonds.

3 **Fulfillment of Psychological Needs:** Relationships fulfill various psychological needs such as the need for intimacy, companionship, and validation. Interacting with others satisfies our innate desire for social interaction and connection.

4 **Shared Experiences:** Humans are wired to seek out shared experiences. Whether it's celebrating successes or navigating challenges together, sharing experiences strengthens the bond between individuals

and creates lasting memories.

5 **Mutual Growth and Learning:** Relationships provide opportunities for personal growth and learning. Interacting with others exposes us to different perspectives, challenges our beliefs, and fosters self-improvement.

6 **Physical Intimacy:** Romantic relationships often involve physical intimacy, which fulfills a basic human need for touch and closeness. Physical affection releases hormones like oxytocin, which promote bonding and attachment.

7 **Practical Benefits:** Relationships often come with practical benefits such as shared resources, division of labor, and support in times of need. For example, family members may provide financial assistance or help

with childcare, while friends may offer career advice or professional networking opportunities.

8 **Biological Imperatives:** From an evolutionary standpoint, forming and maintaining relationships is crucial for survival and reproduction. Humans are social creatures, and our evolutionary history has shaped our behavior to prioritize forming connections with others.

The Role of Love

Love plays a central and multifaceted role in relationships, serving as a foundation for emotional connection, support, and growth. Here are several key aspects of love in relationships:

1 **Emotional Connection**: Love fosters a deep emotional bond between partners, creating a sense of intimacy and understanding. This connection allows individuals to feel seen, heard, and accepted by their partner, leading to feelings of security and belonging.

2 **Support and Care**: Love involves caring for and supporting each other through both good times and challenges. Partners provide emotional, physical, and sometimes financial support, creating a sense of partnership and teamwork.

3 **Mutual Respect and Appreciation**: Love involves respecting and appreciating each other's individuality, opinions, and boundaries. Partners value each other's strengths and differences, fostering a sense

of admiration and gratitude.

4 **Communication and Conflict Resolution:** Love encourages open and honest communication, allowing partners to express their thoughts, feelings, and needs freely. It also involves resolving conflicts respectfully, with a focus on understanding each other's perspectives and finding mutually beneficial solutions.

5 **Growth and Development:** Love supports personal growth and development within the relationship. Partners encourage each other to pursue their goals and aspirations, providing encouragement, motivation, and feedback along the way.

6 **Physical Intimacy:** Love often includes physical affection and intimacy, which can range from hugs and kisses to sexual

expression. Physical connection reinforces emotional closeness and strengthens the bond between partners.

7 **Commitment and Loyalty**: Love involves a commitment to the relationship and each other's well-being. Partners prioritize their relationship, remain faithful, and work through challenges together, fostering trust and security.

8 **Joy and Fulfillment**: Love brings joy, happiness, and fulfillment to both partners' lives. Sharing experiences, creating memories, and enjoying each other's company contributes to a sense of fulfillment and satisfaction in the relationship.

Overall, love serves as a guiding force in relationships, enriching the lives of those involved and contributing to their overall well-being and happiness. However, it's important to recognize that love is complex and requires effort, communication, and mutual respect to flourish over time.

Limitless Love

The notion of limitless love is certainly a compelling concept, often associated with the idea of unconditional love. However, it's worth examining whether such love truly exists without any boundaries or limitations.

While it's undeniable that many people, including mothers, exhibit profound and selfless love for their children, the idea of completely limitless love raises some questions.

Human emotions and relationships are complex, influenced by various factors such as personal experiences, cultural norms, and individual capacities. Even the strongest bonds do encounter challenges or limitations, whether due to differences in values, conflicts, or personal boundaries.

Moreover, the very nature of love implies a connection between individuals, which inherently involves a degree of reciprocity and mutual understanding.

Love often involves an exchange of emotions, actions, and care between individuals. It's not just about giving or receiving; it's a mutual exchange where both parties contribute to the relationship. When one person gives love without receiving it in return, the imbalance can strain the relationship and challenge the notion of limitless love.

In addition, Love is built on understanding, empathy, and connection between individuals. Without a mutual understanding of each other's needs, desires, and boundaries, the depth of love can be limited. True love often thrives on a shared understanding and appreciation of each other's perspectives, which may not always be limitless or unconditional.

While a parent's love for their child may seem boundless, it is still influenced by factors such as the child's behavior, choices, or the parent's own emotional well-being.

Additionally, the concept of limitless love appears to romanticize or overlook the realities of human relationships.

Expecting absolute, unconditional love from others or oneself may set unrealistic standards and lead to disappointment or feelings of inadequacy. Absolute, unconditional love implies a level of perfection that is often unattainable in human relationships.

We are complex beings with flaws and limitations, and expecting flawless love from others or from oneself disregards this reality.

Furthermore, expecting absolute, unconditional love can place undue pressure on relationships. It creates an environment where individuals feel they must constantly prove their love or be loved without question, which can be emotionally draining and unsustainable.

In contrast, recognizing and accepting the complexities of human nature allows for more realistic and fulfilling relationships.

Embracing love that is imperfect, conditional, and subject to growth and change allows for genuine connection and understanding. It acknowledges that love, like individuals themselves, is a journey of growth, acceptance, and forgiveness.

Instead of striving for an unattainable ideal of limitless love, perhaps it's more realistic and meaningful to recognize and appreciate the depth and strength of the love that exists within the boundaries of human experience. This fosters greater empathy, understanding, and acceptance in our relationships.

A Nuanced Understanding of Love

Understanding love involves recognizing that it's a multifaceted and complex phenomenon that defies simplistic categorization.

Instead of viewing love as a binary concept - either present or absent, true or false - it's essential to acknowledge the rich diversity of experiences and expressions that fall under its umbrella.

Firstly, it's crucial to understand that love manifests in various forms, ranging from romantic love to familial love, platonic love, and even self-love. Each of these forms can involve different emotions, motivations, and dynamics, and they may intersect and overlap in intricate ways.

For instance, the love between friends can incorporate elements of intimacy, loyalty, and support, similar to romantic love, but without the same romantic or sexual component.

Moreover, love is not static but dynamic, evolving over time in response to changing circumstances, experiences, and personal growth.

What someone perceives as love in one stage of life may differ from how they experience it in another. This fluidity underscores the complexity of love and the need to approach it with openness and flexibility.

Let's consider a hypothetical example:

In adolescence, Sarah might perceive love as intense infatuation and the thrill of butterflies in her stomach when she's around her crush. She might equate love with grand romantic gestures and the idea of finding her soulmate.

However, as Sarah grows older and gains more life experience, her perception of love may shift. She might come to value qualities like trust, communication, and mutual respect in a relationship.

Love for her might evolve into a deeper connection, where companionship, understanding, and shared goals become more important than fleeting romantic gestures.

So, what Sarah perceives as love in her teenage years, filled with excitement and idealized notions, may differ significantly from how she experiences it in adulthood, where it's grounded in a more mature understanding of what love truly entails.

Furthermore, love encompasses a spectrum of emotions beyond just affection and attachment. It can involve joy, passion, empathy, sacrifice, vulnerability, and sometimes even pain or conflict. Recognizing this diversity of emotional experiences allows for a more nuanced understanding of the complexities inherent in relationships.

Additionally, the expression of love is highly contextual, influenced by cultural norms, social expectations, individual personalities, and past experiences.

What may be considered loving behavior in one cultural context might be interpreted differently in another. Similarly, individuals may have unique ways of expressing and receiving love based on their upbringing, values, and communication styles.

For example, one person might express love through acts of service, such as cooking meals or doing chores for their partner, while another might express love through physical touch, such as hugs or holding hands.

Similarly, one person might feel loved when receiving verbal affirmations or compliments, while another might feel loved through quality time spent together, engaging in meaningful conversations or shared activities.

These expressions and preferences can vary widely from person to person, influenced by their upbringing, cultural background, and personal experiences.

Finally, it's important to acknowledge that love is not always inherently positive or healthy. Unhealthy dynamics such as codependency, possessiveness, or manipulation can masquerade as love, leading to confusion and harm.

Understanding the darker aspects of love alongside its more uplifting aspects is essential for cultivating healthy, and balanced relationships.

Chapter 2

Unveiling Imperfections

No matter how strong or seemingly perfect a bond may appear, it is inevitable that imperfections will emerge, manifesting in various forms such as misbehavior, conflicts, or misunderstandings.

At the heart of this truth lies the inherent complexity of human nature. We are all flawed beings, shaped by our unique experiences, perspectives, and emotional landscapes.

These imperfections often surface in our interactions with others, impacting the dynamics of our relationships in both subtle and profound ways.

Misbehavior, whether intentional or unintentional, is a natural expression of our individuality within the context of a relationship. It can range from minor transgressions to more significant breaches of trust, reflecting the inherent tensions that arise when two distinct personalities come together in intimate proximity.

Conflicts, likewise, are an inevitable consequence of the collision between differing needs, desires, and expectations. They can stem from issues as mundane as household chores or as complex as conflicting values and life goals. Yet, they are also opportunities for growth, providing a crucible in which communication, compromise, and understanding can flourish.

In acknowledging the inevitability of imperfections, we dispel the illusion of perfection that often shrouds our relationships. This acceptance fosters a deeper sense of empathy, compassion, and resilience, enabling us to weather the storms that inevitably arise along the journey of shared existence.

Moreover, it is through navigating these imperfections that relationships are strengthened and enriched over time. Each conflict resolved, each misstep forgiven, and each misunderstanding clarified deepens the bonds of trust and intimacy, forging a connection that is resilient in the face of adversity.

Ultimately, it is the imperfections inherent in every relationship that make them uniquely human, giving them depth, richness, and authenticity.

Embracing these imperfections not as obstacles to overcome, but as integral aspects of the web of connection, allows us to cultivate relationships that are truly meaningful and enduring.

Acknowledgment of Imperfections

Acknowledging and accepting imperfections within relationships is not just a pragmatic approach; it's a fundamental aspect of nurturing healthy and fulfilling connections.

Rather than denying or ignoring the inevitable flaws and rough edges that arise, it's imperative to confront them with open eyes and open hearts. Here's why emphasizing this acceptance is so vital:

1 **Honoring Reality**: Relationships are not fairy tales; they're dynamic journeys between imperfect individuals. Acknowledging imperfections is a humble recognition of this reality.

It's an admission that, despite our best intentions, we all have quirks, insecurities, and past wounds that influence our interactions. By acknowledging these imperfections, we create a space where authenticity can thrive.

2 **Fostering Understanding and Empathy**: When we accept imperfections, we cultivate empathy and understanding. Rather than judging or blaming each other for shortcomings, we strive to comprehend the underlying reasons behind behaviors and

emotions.

This empathy strengthens the emotional bond between partners, fostering a deeper sense of connection and intimacy.

3 **Promoting Growth and Resilience**: In any relationship, challenges are inevitable. Embracing imperfections means confronting these challenges head-on rather than avoiding them.

By acknowledging areas for growth and improvement, couples can work together to overcome obstacles and strengthen their bond. This proactive approach promotes resilience and fortifies the relationship against future hardships.

4 **Building Trust and Vulnerability**: Trust is the cornerstone of any healthy relationship, and vulnerability is its currency.

When we acknowledge imperfections, we demonstrate vulnerability by revealing our true selves to our partners. This vulnerability builds trust over time, as it shows that we are willing to be authentic and transparent in our interactions.

5 **Cultivating Gratitude and Appreciation:** Paradoxically, accepting imperfections can deepen appreciation for our partners' strengths and virtues.

When we recognize and embrace each other's flaws, we gain a newfound appreciation for the unique qualities that make our partners who they are. This gratitude fosters a positive outlook on the relationship and reinforces feelings of love and admiration.

6 **Creating a Culture of Forgiveness**: No relationship is immune to conflict or mistakes. However, by accepting imperfections, couples create a culture of forgiveness and grace.

Rather than holding grudges or dwelling on past wrongs, they can approach conflicts with empathy and a willingness to forgive. This fosters a sense of mutual respect and allows the relationship to move forward with greater harmony and understanding.

Chapter 3

Boundary in Relationship

Boundaries in relationships are like the invisible lines that define where one person ends and another begins. They encompass physical, emotional, and psychological limits that individuals establish to protect their autonomy, well-being, and identity within the relationship.

Healthy boundaries are essential for fostering mutual respect, trust, and intimacy, while also preventing resentment, conflict, and emotional harm.

Firstly, establishing boundaries involves self-awareness and understanding one's own needs, values, and limits. This self-awareness forms the foundation for communicating boundaries effectively to your partner.

It's important to recognize that boundaries may vary from person to person and from relationship to relationship, and they can evolve over time as individuals grow and circumstances change.

In romantic relationships, boundaries might include aspects such as personal space, privacy, and autonomy. For example, individuals may set boundaries around how much time they need alone or with friends, how they share finances or household responsibilities, and what level of physical intimacy they're comfortable with.

Communicating these boundaries openly and respectfully allows both partners to understand and honor each other's needs and preferences.

Emotional boundaries are also crucial in relationships. This involves setting limits on how much emotional responsibility one person should bear for the other, respecting each other's feelings and opinions, and refraining from manipulation or coercion.

Healthy emotional boundaries allow individuals to express themselves authentically without fear of judgment or rejection, while also respecting their partner's autonomy and emotional well-being.

Additionally, boundaries help define acceptable behavior within the relationship. This includes establishing guidelines for communication, resolving conflicts constructively, and addressing issues such as jealousy, possessiveness, or controlling behavior.

By setting clear boundaries around respect, honesty, and trust, couples can create a safe and supportive environment where both partners feel valued and understood.

However, it's important to note that boundaries are not static and may need to be renegotiated as the relationship evolves.

Types of Boundaries

Here are some different types of boundaries that can exist in various relationships:

1 **Physical Boundaries**: These boundaries define the level of physical contact that is acceptable in a relationship. This includes personal space, hugs, kisses, and other forms of physical intimacy. Each person may

have different comfort levels, so it's crucial to respect and communicate about physical boundaries.

2 **Emotional Boundaries**: Emotional boundaries involve the separation between one's emotions and the emotions of others. It's about recognizing and respecting each other's feelings without feeling responsible for them.

Healthy emotional boundaries involve being able to empathize with others while also maintaining a sense of self and not taking on their emotional burdens.

3 **Intellectual Boundaries**: Intellectual boundaries involve respecting each other's thoughts, opinions, and ideas.

It's important to engage in open-minded discussions without dismissing or belittling each other's perspectives. Respecting intellectual boundaries means valuing each other's intellect and allowing for constructive dialogue.

4 **Time Boundaries**: Time boundaries involve respecting each other's time and commitments. This includes being punctual, honoring agreed-upon schedules, and not monopolizing each other's time without consent. Respecting time boundaries demonstrates consideration and reliability in a relationship.

5 **Digital Boundaries**: In the age of technology, digital boundaries have become increasingly important. This includes respecting each other's privacy online, discussing the sharing of digital information, and establishing guidelines for

communication via text, social media, and other digital platforms.

6 **Material Boundaries**: Material boundaries involve respecting each other's belongings, finances, and personal space. This includes asking for permission before borrowing items, respecting financial agreements, and maintaining boundaries around personal possessions.

7 **Sexual Boundaries**: Sexual boundaries involve respecting each other's desires, limits, and consent regarding sexual activity. It's crucial to communicate openly about sexual preferences, boundaries, and consent to ensure that both partners feel safe and comfortable in intimate situations.

8 **Social Boundaries**: Social boundaries involve respecting each other's relationships with

friends, family, and acquaintances. This includes discussing expectations around socializing with others, respecting each other's social plans, and setting boundaries around interactions with ex-partners or other potentially sensitive relationships.

Boundary Violation

Boundary violation occurs when one individual disregards or crosses the personal limits or boundaries of another person, leading to discomfort, distress, or harm. These violations can manifest in various contexts, including interpersonal relationships, professional settings, or societal interactions.

In personal relationships, boundary violations often occur when one party ignores or dismisses the other's expressed needs, desires, or limits. This can take the form of emotional manipulation, coercion, or control, where one person exerts power over the other to satisfy their own needs without regard for the other's autonomy or well-being.

For example, a partner who constantly monitors or restricts their significant other's communication or activities may be guilty of violating boundaries, eroding trust and fostering feelings of suffocation or resentment.

In professional settings, boundary violations can occur between colleagues, supervisors, or clients, compromising the integrity of the work environment and interpersonal dynamics.

This may include instances of harassment, exploitation, or breaches of confidentiality, where individuals exploit their positions of authority or access to information for personal gain or to exert control over others.

For instance, a manager who regularly belittles or intimidates their subordinates may create a hostile work environment that undermines productivity and morale, while also infringing on the rights and dignity of their employees.

Moreover, societal norms and power structures can perpetuate systemic boundary violations, particularly against marginalized or vulnerable populations.

Discrimination, prejudice, and institutionalized oppression can systematically erode individuals' autonomy and agency, limiting their access to resources, opportunities, and basic rights.

Addressing boundary violations requires a multifaceted approach that prioritizes awareness, education, and accountability.

The Consequences of Crossing Boundaries

Crossing boundaries can have a range of consequences, depending on the context and the parties involved. Here are some general consequences to consider:

1 **Trust Issues:** One of the primary consequences of crossing boundaries is a breach of trust.

When someone violates established boundaries, it can erode trust in relationships, whether it's personal, professional, or societal. Trust is the foundation of any healthy relationship, and once it's damaged, it can be challenging to rebuild.

2 **Conflict and Tension**: Crossing boundaries often leads to conflict and tension between individuals or groups. This can result from feelings of violation, disrespect, or a lack of consideration for others' feelings or rights.

3 **Emotional Impact**: Boundary violations can have significant emotional consequences for both parties involved. The person whose boundaries were crossed may experience feelings of anger, resentment, or hurt, while the person who crossed the boundary may feel guilty, ashamed, or confused. Managing these emotions effectively is crucial for maintaining healthy relationships.

4 **Damage to Relationships:** Continual boundary violations can damage relationships beyond repair. Whether it's a friendship, romantic relationship, or professional partnership, repeated breaches of trust and respect can lead to estrangement and ultimately, the breakdown of the relationship.

5 **Legal Ramifications:** In some cases, crossing certain boundaries can have legal consequences. For example, harassment, invasion of privacy, and trespassing are all boundary violations that can result in legal action. It's essential to understand and respect both social and legal boundaries to avoid these repercussions.

6 **Loss of Respect and Credibility:** Consistently crossing boundaries can result in a loss of

respect and credibility from others. Whether it's in personal or professional settings, people are less likely to trust or collaborate with someone who demonstrates a pattern of disregarding boundaries.

7 **Self-Reflection and Growth Opportunities**: On the flip side, experiencing or realizing that you've crossed a boundary can be an opportunity for self-reflection and growth. It allows individuals to examine their behavior, motivations, and impact on others, leading to personal development and improved interpersonal skills.

8 **Setting Precedents**: Crossing boundaries can set precedents for future interactions. If boundaries are not respected, others may feel justified in doing the same, leading to a cycle of escalating boundary violations.

Conversely, enforcing boundaries sets a standard for respectful behavior and establishes healthy boundaries for future interactions.

Enforcing Your Boundary

Enforcing boundaries is crucial for maintaining healthy relationships and self-respect. Here are some steps to help you enforce your boundaries effectively:

1 **Know Your Boundaries:** Before you can enforce your boundaries, you need to know what they are. Take some time to reflect on your values, needs, and limits in various areas of your life, such as work, relationships, and personal space.

2 **Communicate Clearly:** Once you're clear about your boundaries, communicate them

clearly and directly to the people involved. Use "I" statements to express your feelings and needs without blaming or accusing others. For example, say, "I feel uncomfortable when..." or "I need..." This helps others understand where you're coming from and why your boundaries are important to you.

3 **Be Assertive:** Assertiveness is about standing up for yourself and expressing your needs and boundaries confidently and respectfully.

Practice assertive communication techniques, such as maintaining eye contact, using a firm but calm tone of voice, and staying focused on the issue at hand.

4 **Set Consequences:** It's essential to establish consequences for when your boundaries are

violated. Make sure these consequences are reasonable and enforceable.

For example, if someone repeatedly disrespects your boundaries, you might need to limit your interactions with them or seek support from a mediator or counselor.

5 **Follow Through:** Consistency is key when enforcing boundaries. If you don't follow through with the consequences you've set, others may not take your boundaries seriously. Be prepared to enforce your boundaries consistently, even if it's uncomfortable or difficult.

6 **Take Care of Yourself:** Enforcing boundaries can be emotionally challenging, especially if you're met with resistance or pushback. Remember to prioritize self-care and seek support from trusted friends, family

members, or a therapist if you need it.

7 **Practice Self-Compassion:** It's normal to feel guilty or anxious when enforcing boundaries, especially if you're not used to prioritizing your own needs. Practice self-compassion and remind yourself that setting and enforcing boundaries is an essential part of self-care and maintaining healthy relationships.

8 **Reevaluate and Adjust:** Boundaries aren't set in stone and may need to be adjusted over time. Periodically reevaluate your boundaries and make adjustments as needed based on your changing needs and circumstances.

Addressing Boundary Violation

Addressing boundary violations requires a combination of assertiveness, clear communication, and respect for oneself and others. Here's a step-by-step approach:

1 **Identify the Boundary Violation:** Recognize when your boundaries have been crossed. This could be someone invading your personal space, asking inappropriate questions, or disregarding your consent.

2 **Assess the Situation:** Consider the context and severity of the violation. Is it a one-time occurrence or part of a pattern? Is it unintentional or deliberate? This understanding will inform how you approach addressing it.

3 **Check In With Yourself:** Before addressing the issue, take a moment to ground

yourself. Validate your feelings and remind yourself that it's okay to assert your boundaries.

4 **Communicate Clearly:** Approach the person in a calm and assertive manner. Use "I" statements to express how their behavior made you feel and what specific boundary was crossed. For example, "I felt uncomfortable when you commented on my appearance."

5 **Set Clear Expectations:** Clearly state what behavior is unacceptable and what you expect moving forward. Be firm but respectful. For instance, "I need you to respect my personal space and refrain from touching me without my consent."

6 **Listen to Their Response:** Allow the other person to share their perspective. They may

not have been aware that they were crossing a boundary or may have misunderstood the situation.

7 **Establish Consequences:** If the boundary violation persists, clearly communicate the consequences. This could involve limiting contact, seeking support from a supervisor or authority figure, or ending the relationship altogether.

8 **Follow Through:** Consistently enforce your boundaries. If the person continues to disregard them, be prepared to take further action to protect yourself.

9 **Seek Support if Needed:** If you're struggling to address the violation on your own, seek support from friends, family, or a therapist. They can offer guidance and help you navigate the situation.

10 **Reflect on the Outcome:** After addressing the boundary violation, take time to reflect on the outcome and how you feel. Celebrate your courage in standing up for yourself, and consider what you've learned from the experience to better enforce your boundaries in the future.

Consequences for Boundary Violations

Consequences for boundary violations can vary depending on the nature of the relationship and the severity of the violation. Here are some examples across different types of relationships:

1 **Workplace Setting:**

Verbal Warning: For minor violations such as inappropriate language or behavior, a verbal warning may be issued to the employee.

Written Warning: More serious violations, such as harassment or discrimination, may result in a written warning being placed in the employee's file.

Training or Counseling: Employees may be required to undergo training or counseling sessions to address the behavior that led to the violation.

Suspension or Termination: In cases of repeated or severe violations, suspension or termination of employment may be necessary.

2 **Friendships**:

Open Communication: Friends may have a conversation to discuss the boundary violation, express how it made them feel, and work towards resolving the issue.

Temporary Distance: In some cases, friends may choose to take a temporary break from the relationship to allow both parties to reflect on the situation and cool off.

Apology and Making Amends: The individual who violated the boundary may apologize and take steps to make amends, such as changing their behavior or offering support to their friend.

Reevaluation of the Friendship: Depending on the severity of the violation and the response to it, friends may reassess the nature of their relationship and whether it's healthy to continue.

3 **Romantic Relationships:**

Setting Clear Expectations: Couples may establish clear boundaries and expectations for behavior within the relationship.

Temporary Separation: In cases of significant boundary violations, couples may choose to take a temporary break to reassess the relationship and determine next steps.

Couples Counseling: Couples may seek professional help to address underlying issues and improve communication and boundaries within the relationship.

Reconciliation or Separation: Depending on the outcome of discussions and efforts to address the violation, the couple may choose to reconcile and work on rebuilding trust or decide to end the relationship.

4 **Family Relationships:**

Family Meeting: In cases where a boundary violation affects multiple family members, a family meeting may be called to discuss the issue openly and find a resolution.

Time Apart: Family members may take some time apart to cool off and reflect on the situation before coming together to address the violation.

Seeking Therapy: Family therapy can provide a safe space for all members to express their feelings and concerns and work towards healing and reconciliation.

Setting Boundaries: Clear boundaries may be established or reinforced to prevent similar violations from occurring in the future.

Chapter 4

Acknowledging Fallout

Acknowledging fallout in relationships is crucial because it acknowledges the impact of actions on trust and boundaries. When trust is compromised or boundaries are crossed, fallout is inevitable.

Ignoring or downplaying this fallout can exacerbate existing issues and hinder the process of healing and rebuilding the relationship.

Firstly, acknowledging fallout demonstrates respect for the affected parties' emotions and experiences. It validates their feelings of hurt, betrayal, or discomfort, showing that their concerns are heard and understood. This acknowledgment opens the door for honest communication, which is essential for repairing the damage done to trust and boundaries.

Secondly, acknowledging fallout helps prevent further harm to the relationship. By recognizing the consequences of actions, individuals can take responsibility for their behavior and work towards addressing the underlying issues.

Ignoring fallout may lead to a cycle of resentment, avoidance, or repeated transgressions, further eroding trust and deepening the rift between partners.

Moreover, acknowledging fallout fosters accountability and accountability is necessary for rebuilding trust. When individuals take ownership of their actions and their impact on others, it demonstrates a willingness to repair the damage and invest in the relationship's well-being. This can pave the way for meaningful apologies, reparative actions, and mutual efforts to establish clearer boundaries and rebuild trust.

In relationships where trust and boundaries are tested, acknowledging fallout is a necessary step towards growth and reconciliation. It signals a commitment to addressing problems head-on and working through challenges together.

By facing the fallout with honesty and empathy, individuals can lay the groundwork for a stronger, healthier relationship built on trust, respect, and mutual understanding.

Steps to Acknowledge Fallout

Acknowledging fallout, whether it's from a personal situation or a broader issue, involves several steps to address and mitigate its effects. Here's a breakdown of those steps:

1 **Recognize the Fallout:** The first step is to acknowledge that fallout has occurred. This involves being aware of the consequences, whether they are emotional, social, or practical.

2 **Assess the Situation:** Understand the scope and impact of the fallout. This involves evaluating who or what is affected, the severity of the consequences, and any immediate actions that need to be taken.

3 **Take Responsibility:** Accept accountability for any role you may have played in causing or contributing to the fallout. Taking

responsibility is crucial for moving forward constructively.

4 **Communicate Openly:** Honest communication is key in addressing fallout. Be transparent about what has happened, its implications, and how you plan to address it. This applies to both personal and professional situations.

5 **Apologize if Necessary:** If your actions directly caused harm or contributed to the fallout, offer a sincere apology. Acknowledge the impact on others and express remorse for any pain or inconvenience caused.

6 **Address Immediate Needs:** Attend to any urgent needs or concerns resulting from the fallout. This might involve providing support, resources, or assistance to those

affected.

7 **Develop a Plan**: Create a strategy for addressing the fallout and mitigating its effects in the short and long term. Identify specific steps, allocate resources, and set realistic goals for recovery.

8 **Implement Solutions**: Put your plan into action, addressing issues systematically and proactively. This may involve making changes, resolving conflicts, or providing support as needed.

9 **Monitor Progress**: Continuously assess the effectiveness of your actions and adjust your approach as necessary. Stay vigilant for any new challenges or developments that may arise.

10   **Learn and Grow**: Use the experience as an

opportunity for personal or organizational growth. Reflect on what you've learned from the fallout and how you can prevent similar issues in the future.

Chapter 5

Lesson in Accountability

Accountability is about more than just admitting when we make mistakes. It's about recognizing the role we play in shaping our own lives and the lives of those around us. When we hold ourselves accountable, we take ownership of our actions, decisions, and their outcomes.

Accountability is crucial in various aspects of life, from personal relationships to professional environments and governance systems.

Here are some key reasons why accountability is important:

1 **Trust and Credibility**: In any relationship or organization, accountability fosters trust and credibility. When individuals or entities hold themselves accountable for their actions and decisions, it demonstrates reliability and integrity, which are essential for building trust among peers, colleagues, customers, and the public.

2 **Responsibility and Ownership**: Accountability encourages individuals to take ownership of their actions, behaviors, and outcomes. It instills a sense of responsibility where individuals understand that they are answerable for the consequences of their choices and actions. This mindset promotes proactive problem-solving and a commitment to achieving goals.

3 **Performance and Productivity**: When individuals know they are accountable for their performance and outcomes, they are more likely to strive for excellence and productivity. Accountability creates a framework for setting clear expectations, measuring progress, and providing feedback, which helps identify areas for improvement and encourages continuous growth and development.

4 **Ethical Behavior and Integrity**: A culture of accountability promotes ethical behavior and integrity within an organization or community. When individuals are held accountable for adhering to ethical standards and organizational values, it helps prevent misconduct, fraud, and unethical practices.

It also reinforces the importance of honesty, fairness, and transparency in decision-making processes.

5 **Learning and Improvement**: Embracing accountability involves acknowledging mistakes, learning from failures, and using feedback to make necessary adjustments. It creates a culture where individuals are encouraged to reflect on their experiences, identify areas for improvement, and take proactive measures to enhance their skills and performance.

This continuous learning and improvement cycle are essential for personal and professional growth.

6 **Effective Decision-Making**: Accountability facilitates effective decision-making processes by ensuring that decisions are

made thoughtfully, based on reliable information, and aligned with organizational objectives.

When individuals are accountable for their decisions, they are more likely to consider the potential consequences, seek input from relevant stakeholders, and evaluate alternative options before taking action.

7 **Legal and Regulatory Compliance**: In many contexts, accountability is a legal and regulatory requirement. Organizations, institutions, and public officials are often mandated to comply with laws, regulations, and industry standards, and being held accountable ensures adherence to these requirements.

Failure to uphold accountability may lead to legal consequences, financial penalties, and reputational damage.

Practicing Accountability

Practicing accountability involves adopting certain behaviors and habits that promote responsibility, integrity, and transparency. Here are some steps to help you cultivate accountability in your personal and professional life:

1 **Reflect on Your Actions:** Take time to reflect on your actions and their consequences. Ask yourself how your choices have impacted others and what you can do to make amends if necessary.

2 **Own Your Mistakes:** When you make a mistake, resist the urge to shift blame or make excuses. Instead, take ownership of your actions and apologize if necessary. This

demonstrates humility and sincerity.

3 **Set Clear Expectations:** Clearly define roles, responsibilities, and expectations in any group or team setting. This helps ensure that everyone understands their role in achieving shared goals and holds each other accountable.

4 **Communicate Effectively:** Foster open and honest communication within your personal and professional relationships. Encourage feedback and constructive criticism, and be receptive to it.

5 **Follow Through:** Hold yourself accountable for following through on your commitments. If you promise to do something, make sure you deliver on your word. This builds credibility and reliability.

6 **Seek Feedback and Input**: Actively seek feedback from peers, colleagues, mentors, and stakeholders to evaluate your performance and identify areas for improvement. Be receptive to constructive criticism and use it as an opportunity for growth and development.

Solicit input from others when making important decisions to gain diverse perspectives and insights.

7 **Hold Yourself and Others Accountable**: Hold yourself and others accountable for meeting agreed-upon standards, deadlines, and expectations. Establish clear consequences for failing to fulfill responsibilities or achieve objectives, but also provide support and resources to help individuals succeed.

Lead by example and demonstrate your commitment to accountability in your actions and behaviors.

8 **Track Progress and Evaluate Results**: Regularly monitor your progress towards your goals and objectives. Keep track of key performance indicators, milestones, and metrics to assess your effectiveness and identify areas for improvement.

Reflect on your achievements and setbacks, and use this information to make informed decisions and adjust your strategies as needed.

Chapter 6

The Limits of Manipulation

Manipulation in relationships and interactions can be a delicate and sometimes harmful practice. It involves exerting influence over others in subtle or deceptive ways to achieve a desired outcome, often at the expense of the other person's autonomy or well-being.

Here are some aspects to consider when discussing this practice:

1 **Understanding Manipulation**: Manipulation can take various forms, including guilt-tripping, gaslighting, withholding information, or using flattery to gain favor. It's often about controlling the narrative or

the emotions of others to serve one's own interests.

2 **Motivations Behind Manipulation**: People may resort to manipulation for a variety of reasons, such as insecurity, a desire for power or control, fear of rejection, or a need to protect oneself from perceived threats. Understanding these underlying motivations can shed light on why someone engages in manipulative behavior.

3 **Impact on Relationships**: Manipulation erodes trust and undermines the foundation of healthy relationships. It can create a dynamic of fear, resentment, and manipulation cycles, where both parties feel the need to manipulate to get their needs met. Over time, this can lead to emotional distancing and even the breakdown of the

relationship.

4 **Recognizing Manipulative Tactics**: Being able to recognize manipulation is crucial for protecting oneself from its negative effects. This includes being aware of red flags such as inconsistency in words and actions, feeling constantly guilty or inadequate, or experiencing a sense of confusion or doubt in the relationship.

5 **Setting Boundaries**: Establishing and maintaining clear boundaries is essential for preventing manipulation from taking hold in relationships. This involves knowing one's own values, needs, and limits, and communicating them assertively to others.

6 **Building Healthy Communication Skills**: Healthy communication is the antidote to manipulation. It involves active listening,

empathy, honesty, and transparency. By fostering open and honest dialogue, individuals can build trust and mutual respect in their relationships.

7 **Seeking Support**: If manipulation is present in a relationship, seeking support from a trusted friend, family member, or therapist can be invaluable. Having an outside perspective can help individuals recognize manipulative patterns and develop strategies for addressing them effectively.

8 **Personal Growth and Self-Reflection**: Ultimately, overcoming manipulation requires a commitment to personal growth and self-reflection. This may involve exploring one's own insecurities and vulnerabilities, learning healthier ways of relating to others, and cultivating empathy

and compassion.

Ethical Considerations

Whether it's in personal relationships, business negotiations, or broader societal contexts, manipulation raises significant moral concerns.

First and foremost, manipulation undermines the autonomy and agency of the individuals being manipulated. When someone is deceived or coerced into making a decision, their ability to freely choose what is genuinely in their best interest is compromised.

This erodes the foundation of trust and mutual respect that is essential for healthy relationships and societal interactions.

Moreover, manipulation often involves exploiting vulnerabilities or weaknesses in others. This can lead to feelings of betrayal, resentment, and psychological harm. It preys on people's emotions and insecurities, manipulating them into doing things they might not otherwise do if they had full information and agency.

In essence, it takes advantage of asymmetries in power dynamics and information to serve the manipulator's interests at the expense of others.

From a broader societal perspective, a culture of manipulation can corrode the fabric of trust and cooperation essential for a functioning society. When people feel constantly manipulated or deceived, they may become cynical and disengaged, leading to a breakdown in social cohesion and cooperation.

On the other hand, some might argue that manipulation is a necessary tool in certain contexts, such as marketing or negotiation. They might contend that persuasion tactics, even if they involve some level of manipulation, are simply part of the competitive nature of these arenas.

However, even in these contexts, there are ethical boundaries that should not be crossed. Manipulation that crosses into deception or coercion is morally indefensible, regardless of the context.

Ultimately, the ethical implications of manipulation urge us to consider the broader consequences of our actions on others.

Instead of resorting to deceptive tactics to achieve our goals, we should strive for transparency, honesty, and empathy in our interactions with others. Building trust and fostering genuine connections not only leads to more fulfilling relationships but also contributes to a healthier and more ethical society as a whole.

Alternatives to Manipulation

Promoting healthier alternatives to manipulation is essential for fostering trust, understanding, and genuine connections in relationships. Here are some key alternatives:

1 **Open Communication**: Encourage open and honest communication between partners. Create a safe space where both individuals feel comfortable expressing their thoughts, feelings, and concerns without fear of judgment or retaliation. This allows for transparency and helps resolve conflicts

constructively.

2 **Honesty**: Cultivate a culture of honesty and integrity in the relationship. Be truthful with each other, even when it's difficult. Honesty builds trust and strengthens the bond between partners, laying a foundation for a healthy and resilient relationship.

3 **Mutual Respect**: Show respect for each other's boundaries, opinions, and autonomy. Recognize and appreciate each other's strengths, differences, and individuality. Respectful behavior fosters a sense of equality and partnership, rather than power dynamics based on manipulation.

4 **Empathy and Understanding**: Practice empathy and seek to understand your partner's perspective. Put yourself in their

shoes and validate their emotions and experiences. Empathetic listening promotes empathy and deepens emotional connection.

5 **Consent and Consent Culture**: Prioritize consent in all aspects of the relationship, whether it's physical intimacy, decision-making, or personal boundaries. Respect each other's autonomy and always seek enthusiastic consent before engaging in any activity.

6 **Conflict Resolution Skills**: Learn and practice healthy conflict resolution skills, such as active listening, compromise, and problem-solving. Approach conflicts as opportunities for growth and understanding rather than opportunities for manipulation or control.

7 **Boundaries**: Establish and respect clear boundaries within the relationship. Boundaries define what acceptable and unacceptable behavior is. This helps to prevent manipulation and maintain mutual respect.

8 **Self-awareness and Self-reflection**: Cultivate self-awareness and self-reflection to recognize and address any manipulative tendencies or unhealthy patterns in yourself. Take responsibility for your actions and strive to improve communication and behavior.

Reflection

It's crucial for each of us to take a moment for introspection, to honestly assess our tendencies towards manipulation in our interactions with others.

Manipulation can sometimes be subtle, creeping into our words and actions without us even realizing it. But by shining a light on these behaviors, we can start to cultivate healthier, more authentic relationships.

Consider your communication style. Are you always trying to steer conversations in a certain direction? Do you find yourself using guilt or flattery to get what you want? These are signs that manipulation might be at play. Reflect on why you feel the need to manipulate situations or people. Is it driven by fear, insecurity, or a desire for control?

Instead of resorting to manipulation, strive for open and honest communication. Be transparent about your intentions and respect the autonomy of others. Authentic relationships are built on trust and mutual understanding, not on manipulation and deceit.

Take the time to listen actively to others, without an agenda or ulterior motive. Practice empathy and strive to understand their perspectives. When conflicts arise, address them directly and constructively, rather than resorting to manipulation tactics to get your way.

Ultimately, fostering healthier, more authentic relationships requires self-awareness, empathy, and a commitment to integrity. By being mindful of our tendencies towards manipulation and actively working to overcome them, we can cultivate deeper connections based on trust, respect, and genuine care.

Avoiding Manipulation

Avoiding manipulation and fostering genuine connections requires awareness, empathy, and clear boundaries. Here are some practical tips:

1 **Trust Your Instincts**: If something feels off in a relationship or interaction, trust your gut. Don't dismiss red flags or doubts.

2 **Develop Emotional Intelligence**: Understand your own emotions and motivations, as well as those of others. This helps you discern genuine intentions from manipulative ones.

3 **Set Boundaries**: Clearly communicate your boundaries and respect others' boundaries too. Healthy relationships are built on mutual respect and understanding.

4 **Be Authentic**: Be yourself in all interactions. Authenticity attracts genuine connections while repelling manipulative ones.

5 **Listen Actively**: Practice active listening by giving your full attention to others without interrupting or judging. This fosters trust and deeper connections.

6 **Ask Questions**: Show genuine interest in others by asking open-ended questions and being curious about their experiences, thoughts, and feelings.

7 **Pay Attention to Actions, Not Just Words**: Actions speak louder than words. Pay attention to how people behave over time,

as it often reveals their true intentions.

8 **Educate Yourself**: Learn about manipulation tactics and psychological principles. Knowledge is power when it comes to protecting yourself from manipulation.

9 **Surround Yourself with Positive Influences**: Spend time with people who uplift and support you genuinely. Positive relationships reinforce authenticity and discourage manipulation.

10 **Practice Self-Care**: Take care of your physical, emotional, and mental well-being. When you prioritize self-care, you become more resilient against manipulation and can engage in healthier relationships.

11 **Be Assertive**: Stand up for yourself respectfully and assertively when needed. Don't be afraid to say no or express your

needs and preferences.

12 **Evaluate Relationships Regularly**: Reflect on your relationships periodically to assess their health and whether they align with your values and goals.

By integrating these practices into your daily interactions and relationships, you can navigate away from manipulation and nurture authentic connections built on trust, respect, and mutual understanding.

Chapter 7

Wisdom in Navigating Relationships

Wisdom in navigating relationships encompasses a multifaceted understanding of oneself, others, and the dynamics at play within any given relationship.

At its core, wisdom in this context involves the ability to cultivate empathy, emotional intelligence, and perspective-taking skills. It goes beyond mere knowledge or intelligence, delving into the realm of insight and discernment.

Firstly, wisdom in relationships involves self-awareness, which is crucial for understanding one's own needs, desires, and boundaries. By being in tune with our own emotions and motivations, we can better communicate them to others and make conscious choices that align with our values.

Additionally, self-awareness enables us to recognize and work on our own shortcomings and areas for growth, fostering personal development that positively impacts our relationships.

Secondly, wisdom in relationships entails empathy and compassion towards others. It involves the ability to put oneself in another's shoes, understand their perspectives, and validate their experiences.

Empathetic listening, genuine curiosity, and non-judgmental communication are key components of this aspect of wisdom. By fostering empathy, individuals can build deeper connections with others, resolve conflicts more effectively, and create a supportive and nurturing environment within their relationships.

Finally, wisdom in navigating relationships involves the ability to discern when to hold on and when to let go. This requires a balance between commitment and flexibility, knowing when to invest time and energy into nurturing a relationship and when it may be healthier to move on.

Wisdom allows individuals to recognize toxic or unhealthy dynamics and make decisions that prioritize their well-being and growth. It involves learning from past experiences, being open to change, and continually adapting to the evolving nature of relationships.

The Need for Discernment

Discernment plays a crucial role in the success and well-being of relationships, as it involves the ability to judge situations accurately and make wise choices. Here are some key points highlighting the importance of discernment in relationships:

1 **Understanding Reality:** Discernment enables individuals to see situations and people for what they truly are, rather than being swayed by emotions or external influences. This clear perception is essential for building authentic and healthy relationships based on a realistic understanding of each other.

2 **Effective Communication:** Discernment contributes to effective communication

within relationships. It helps individuals distinguish between what is said and what is meant, promoting open and honest dialogues. Misunderstandings and conflicts are minimized when both parties can accurately interpret each other's intentions.

3 **Identifying Red Flags:** Discernment empowers individuals to recognize potential problems or red flags early in a relationship. Whether it's identifying toxic behaviors, dishonesty, or incompatibility, having a discerning eye allows individuals to make informed decisions about the viability and health of a relationship.

4 **Conflict Resolution:** When conflicts arise, discernment plays a crucial role in finding constructive solutions. Individuals with strong discernment can navigate through

misunderstandings, identify the root causes of conflicts, and make wise decisions on how to address and resolve them, fostering growth and understanding within the relationship.

5 **Personal Boundaries:** Discernment helps in establishing and maintaining healthy personal boundaries. Being able to recognize when one's limits are being pushed or crossed allows individuals to assert themselves appropriately, ensuring that relationships remain respectful and balanced.

6 **Decision-Making in Relationships:** Whether it's choosing a life partner, deciding on shared goals, or navigating major life changes, discernment guides individuals in making choices that align with their values

and long-term aspirations. This ability to make wise decisions contributes to the overall success and fulfillment of the relationship.

7 **Emotional Well-being:** Discernment is closely linked to emotional intelligence. Understanding one's own emotions and those of a partner is essential for creating a supportive and emotionally healthy relationship. It enables individuals to respond appropriately to various situations, fostering emotional well-being for both partners.

How to Discern the Nature and Quality of Your Relationship

Discerning the nature and quality of your relationship is an important aspect of personal growth and ensuring that you're investing your time and emotions wisely. Here are some steps to help you properly discern your relationship:

1 **Reflect on Your Feelings:** Take some time to introspect and evaluate your feelings towards the relationship. Are you genuinely happy and fulfilled, or do you often feel conflicted, stressed, or unhappy?

2 **Communication:** Open and honest communication is key to understanding where you stand in your relationship. Have candid conversations with your partner about your thoughts, feelings, and

expectations for the relationship.

3 **Assess Compatibility**: Evaluate whether you and your partner share common values, goals, and interests. While differences can be enriching, fundamental incompatibilities may lead to long-term challenges.

4 **Observe Behavior**: Pay attention to how your partner treats you and others. Do they show respect, empathy, and support? Or do they display behaviors that are hurtful, disrespectful, or manipulative?

5 **Consider Long-term Goals**: Think about whether your relationship aligns with your long-term goals and aspirations. Are you both committed to similar paths, such as marriage, children, career ambitions, or lifestyle choices?

6 **Seek Advice**: Sometimes, an outside perspective can provide valuable insights. Consider seeking advice from trusted friends, family members, or even a therapist who can offer objective guidance.

7 **Evaluate Trust and Communication**: Trust and communication are the foundation of a healthy relationship. Assess whether you feel secure and valued in your relationship, and whether there are any significant trust issues or communication barriers.

8 **Listen to Your Intuition**: Trust your instincts. If something feels off or if you have persistent doubts about the relationship, it's essential to address these concerns and explore them further.

9 **Assess Conflict Resolution**: Every relationship encounters conflicts, but it's

crucial to evaluate how you and your partner navigate and resolve disagreements. Healthy conflict resolution involves respect, compromise, and a willingness to work through challenges together.

10   **Take Time to Reflect**: Give yourself space to reflect on the insights you've gathered. It's okay to take time to process your thoughts and emotions before making any decisions about the future of your relationship.

Thoughtful Decision-Making

Thoughtful decision-making in relationships is crucial for fostering healthy dynamics and nurturing strong connections.

When we approach decisions with careful consideration for their potential impact on others, we demonstrate respect, empathy, and maturity. Here are some key reasons why thoughtful decision-making is significant in navigating relationships:

1 **Respect and Empathy**: Thoughtful decision-making is an outward manifestation of respect and empathy towards our partners. It involves considering their feelings, perspectives, and needs as valid and important.

This acknowledgment of their emotional landscape fosters an environment where both individuals feel valued and understood. When we make decisions with empathy, we are more attuned to how our actions may impact our partners emotionally, allowing for greater connection and intimacy.

2 **Maintaining Trust**: Trust is the cornerstone of any healthy relationship. It's built on a foundation of reliability, honesty, and mutual respect. Thoughtful decision-making is essential for preserving and strengthening this trust.

By involving our partners in the decision-making process and considering their feelings and concerns, we demonstrate our commitment to transparency and mutual understanding. This transparency helps to prevent misunderstandings and resentments, creating a safe space where both partners can be vulnerable without fear of judgment or betrayal.

3 **Conflict Resolution**: Conflict is inevitable in any relationship, but how we navigate it can make all the difference. Thoughtful decision-making can serve as a powerful tool for resolving conflicts constructively.

By approaching disagreements with empathy and a willingness to listen, we create an atmosphere of mutual respect and understanding. This allows both partners to express their needs and concerns openly and honestly, paving the way for collaborative problem-solving and compromise.

In this way, thoughtful decision-making transforms conflicts from sources of tension into opportunities for growth and deeper connection.

4 **Long-Term Relationship Satisfaction:** Sustaining a fulfilling and lasting relationship requires ongoing effort and commitment from both partners. Thoughtful decision-making plays a crucial role in this process by fostering emotional intimacy and mutual respect.

When both individuals feel heard, valued, and understood, they are more likely to experience greater satisfaction and fulfillment in their relationship. This sense of satisfaction becomes the bedrock upon which a strong and enduring partnership can thrive, even in the face of challenges and setbacks.

5 **Personal Growth:** Relationships are not just about the connection between two people;

they also provide a fertile ground for personal growth and self-discovery. Thoughtful decision-making invites us to reflect on our own values, beliefs, and behaviors, as well as how they impact our partners.

It challenges us to confront our biases and assumptions, fostering greater self-awareness and empathy in the process. By engaging in this continuous process of self-reflection and improvement, we not only strengthen our relationships but also cultivate a deeper understanding of ourselves and our place in the world.

6 **Impact on Others**: Our decisions have consequences that extend beyond ourselves, affecting the lives of those around us, including our partners.

Thoughtful decision-making requires us to consider the potential impact of our choices on our partners and to weigh their needs and concerns alongside our own.

This awareness of the interconnectedness of our actions fosters a sense of shared responsibility and accountability within the relationship. It reminds us that our decisions have the power to shape the experiences and emotions of those we care about, motivating us to choose wisely and with care.

Examples of Thoughtful Decision Making

Here are examples of thoughtful decision-making in various relationships:

1 **Romantic Relationship**:

Planning surprises: Taking the time to plan a special date or surprise gift tailored to your partner's interests and preferences.

Active listening: Making an effort to actively listen to your partner's concerns, needs, and desires before making decisions that affect both of you.

Considering their feelings: Before making major decisions, such as moving in together or changing jobs, considering how it will impact your partner and discussing it openly with them.

2 **Family Relationship:**

Balancing needs: Considering the needs and schedules of all family members when planning events or vacations.

Respecting boundaries: Being mindful of personal boundaries and respecting them, whether it's regarding personal space, privacy, or emotional needs.

Supporting individual goals: Encouraging and supporting each family member's individual goals and aspirations, even if they differ from your own.

3 **Friendship:**

Checking in: Regularly checking in with friends to see how they're doing and offering support or assistance when needed.

Being reliable: Following through on promises and commitments, and being there for friends during both good times and bad.

Respecting differences: Respecting each other's differences in opinions, beliefs, and lifestyles, even if you don't always agree.

4 Professional Relationship:

Effective communication: Communicating clearly and respectfully with colleagues and supervisors, especially when discussing sensitive topics or conflicts.

Collaboration: Working collaboratively with team members, valuing their input and ideas, and making decisions that benefit the team as a whole.

Recognition and appreciation: Recognizing and appreciating the contributions of others, whether through verbal praise, written acknowledgment, or other forms of recognition.

In each of these examples, thoughtful decision-making involves considering the needs, feelings, and perspectives of the other person or people involved, and making choices that demonstrate care, respect, and empathy.

Chapter 8

Balancing Power and Respect

Maintaining balance in relationships is akin to tending to a delicate ecosystem. Just as in nature, harmony is essential for sustenance and growth.

In any relationship, be it romantic, familial, or professional, balance ensures that each party feels valued and understood.

Central to this equilibrium is respect. Regardless of the roles individuals play within the relationship dynamic, respect serves as the cornerstone upon which everything else is built. It's the mutual recognition of each other's worth, boundaries, and autonomy.

In romantic relationships, balance and respect mean honoring each other's needs and aspirations, communicating openly and honestly, and supporting each other's growth. It's about recognizing that both partners bring unique strengths and perspectives to the table, and neither should dominate or diminish the other.

Within families, balance is essential for fostering healthy dynamics. Parents must respect their children's autonomy and individuality, while children must respect their parents' guidance and wisdom.

Sibling relationships thrive when there's a mutual understanding of each other's differences and a commitment to supporting one another.

Even in professional settings, balance and respect are vital. Colleagues must acknowledge each other's contributions, expertise, and boundaries. Leaders must respect their team members' input and well-being, while employees must respect their supervisors' authority and decisions.

Ultimately, maintaining balance and respect in relationships cultivates trust, intimacy, and resilience. It fosters an environment where individuals feel safe to express themselves authentically and pursue mutual goals together. It's the foundation upon which healthy, fulfilling relationships are built and sustained.

Power Struggles in Various Relationships

Power struggles can emerge in various relationships, both personal and professional. Here are some common situations where power struggles may occur:

1 **Personal Relationships**:

Parent-child dynamics: As children grow into teenagers and adults, they may challenge parental authority, leading to power struggles over decisions, rules, and responsibilities.

Romantic relationships: Power imbalances can arise when one partner seeks to dominate or control the other, leading to conflicts over decision-making, communication, and individual autonomy.

Sibling rivalry: Competing for parental attention, resources, or recognition can create power struggles between siblings, especially if there's a significant age gap or perceived favoritism.

Friendships: Power dynamics can surface when one friend tries to assert dominance or manipulate the other, leading to conflicts over social influence, activities, and loyalty.

2 **Professional Relationships:**

Manager-employee relationships: Power struggles may occur when managers micromanage, withhold resources, or exert undue control over their subordinates, leading to tensions over autonomy, recognition, and career advancement.

Team dynamics: Within teams, power struggles can arise when members vie for leadership positions, control over projects, or credit for achievements, leading to conflicts over decision-making authority and task distribution.

Interdepartmental conflicts: Different departments within an organization may compete for resources, influence, or recognition, leading to power struggles over budget allocation, project prioritization, and strategic direction.

Client-professional relationships: Professionals such as lawyers, consultants, and healthcare providers may experience power struggles with clients who challenge their expertise, demand preferential treatment, or refuse to follow advice, leading to conflicts over boundaries, expectations, and outcomes.

Consequences of Power Imbalances

Exploiting power imbalances within relationships can have profoundly damaging consequences for both parties involved. Here are some negative repercussions:

1 **Emotional Manipulation**: When one partner wields power over the other, they may resort to emotional manipulation tactics to control or coerce the other person into complying with their desires. This can include guilt-tripping, gaslighting, or threatening behavior, all of which can lead to psychological harm and erode the victim's self-esteem.

2 **Loss of Autonomy**: Exploiting power imbalances often results in the oppressed

partner feeling like they have no control over their own lives or decisions. Their autonomy is compromised, leading to feelings of helplessness and dependence on the dominant partner.

3 **Undermined Confidence**: Constantly being subjected to the authority of a more powerful partner can undermine the confidence and self-worth of the oppressed individual. They may begin to doubt their own abilities and judgment, leading to a diminished sense of self.

4 **Isolation**: The dominant partner may intentionally isolate the other person from friends, family, or support networks, further consolidating their power and control. This isolation can leave the oppressed individual feeling trapped and alone, with no one to

turn to for help or perspective.

5 **Physical Harm:** In extreme cases, exploitation of power imbalances can escalate to physical abuse. The dominant partner may use their position of power to inflict harm on the other person without fear of reprisal, leading to serious injury or even death.

6 **Imbalanced Relationship Dynamics:** Exploitation of power imbalances perpetuates unequal relationship dynamics where one person holds all the power and the other person is continually subjugated. This imbalance prevents the relationship from being truly healthy and equitable, leading to resentment and dissatisfaction on both sides.

7 **Long-term Psychological Trauma**: The effects of exploitation within relationships can have long-lasting psychological consequences for both parties. The oppressed individual may suffer from anxiety, depression, PTSD, or other mental health issues, while the dominant partner may also experience guilt, shame, or remorse for their actions.

Overall, exploiting power imbalances within relationships creates a toxic environment that can cause significant harm to both parties involved, undermining trust, respect, and mutual well-being. It's essential for individuals to recognize and address these imbalances to cultivate healthy, equitable relationships built on mutual respect and cooperation.

Fairness and Mutual Understanding

In relationships, fairness and mutual understanding serve as essential pillars, offering a harmonious alternative to the detrimental dynamics of power struggles.

Fairness fosters an environment where both parties feel valued and respected, each person's needs and perspectives considered with equal weight. This principle acknowledges the inherent equality between individuals, emphasizing the importance of equitable treatment and opportunities within the relationship.

When fairness prevails, decisions are made collaboratively, ensuring that neither partner dominates the other.

Mutual understanding complements fairness by nurturing empathy and compassion between partners. It involves actively listening to one another, seeking to comprehend each other's feelings, thoughts, and experiences.

Through genuine empathy, individuals can better appreciate their partner's perspective, even in moments of disagreement or conflict. This understanding builds trust and strengthens the bond between partners, fostering a sense of unity and solidarity.

Moreover, mutual understanding cultivates effective communication, enabling partners to navigate challenges constructively and find mutually beneficial solutions.

By prioritizing fairness and mutual understanding, relationships transcend power struggles, creating space for cooperation, compromise, and growth. Rather than vying for control or dominance, partners collaborate as equals, drawing on their shared values and aspirations to nurture a fulfilling connection.

For example, Sarah and Alex have been in a relationship for several years. Recently, they've been disagreeing more frequently about how to manage their finances.

Sarah prefers to save money for future goals, while Alex enjoys spending on occasional indulgences. Instead of resorting to power struggles or trying to dominate the decision-making process, they decide to sit down and have an open conversation.

During their discussion, they both express their perspectives and listen actively to each other's concerns.

Sarah explains the importance of saving for emergencies and long-term plans, while Alex shares his desire to enjoy some of their earnings in the present moment. They realize that both perspectives are valid and that they can find a middle ground.

Ultimately, they come up with a compromise: they'll allocate a portion of their income for savings and future goals, while also setting aside some money for leisure activities that they both enjoy.

By prioritizing fairness and mutual understanding, Sarah and Alex transcend the power struggle over finances. They collaborate as equals, drawing on their shared values of financial responsibility and enjoyment of life to nurture a fulfilling connection and promote growth in their relationship.

In this context, conflicts become opportunities for learning and strengthening the relationship, rather than sources of resentment or division.

Ultimately, embracing fairness and mutual understanding fosters a relationship built on respect, empathy, and genuine partnership, enriching the lives of both individuals involved.

Chapter 9

Strategies for Success

Maintaining Relationships

Preserving the integrity of relationships while actively pursuing personal goals is not only important; it's essential for a truly fulfilling and balanced life.

Our relationships, whether with family, friends, or romantic partners, provide us with a sense of belonging, support, and emotional nourishment that is invaluable. Neglecting these connections in favor of personal ambitions can lead to feelings of isolation, resentment, and a profound sense of emptiness, despite any successes we may achieve.

When we prioritize the well-being of our relationships alongside our individual goals, we foster an environment of trust, communication, and mutual respect.

Our loved ones become not only our supporters but also our sounding boards, offering valuable insights, perspective, and encouragement along our journey. Their unwavering support can make the pursuit of our goals feel less daunting and more achievable, as we draw strength from their belief in us.

Furthermore, maintaining strong bonds with others serves to enrich our own lives in numerous ways. Emotional connection and intimacy are fundamental human needs, and nurturing these connections contributes significantly to our overall happiness and well-being.

Research has consistently shown that individuals with strong social support networks tend to experience lower levels of stress, anxiety, and depression, and are better equipped to cope with life's challenges.

Moreover, our relationships provide us with opportunities for personal growth and self-discovery. Through interactions with others, we gain valuable insights into ourselves, our values, and our priorities.

The feedback we receive from our loved ones helps us to understand our strengths and weaknesses more fully, allowing us to develop into the best versions of ourselves.

In essence, while personal goals are undoubtedly important and worth pursuing, they should never come at the expense of our relationships. By honoring and preserving the integrity of our connections with others, we enhance our own well-being and contribute to the strength and resilience of our communities.

In this way, our pursuit of personal goals becomes not just a solitary endeavor, but a shared journey enriched by the love, support, and companionship of those we hold dear.

Importance of Compromise

Compromise is the cornerstone of conflict resolution and negotiation, essential for fostering cooperation and achieving mutually beneficial outcomes. Here's why it's so vital:

1 **Balancing Interests:** In any conflict, each party typically has its own set of interests

and priorities. Compromise allows these interests to be balanced, ensuring that neither side completely loses out.

2 **Preserving Relationships:** By finding common ground through compromise, parties can maintain positive relationships even in the face of disagreements. This is particularly important in long-term partnerships or collaborations where ongoing cooperation is necessary.

3 **Enhancing Creativity:** Compromise often requires creative problem-solving to address the needs of all parties involved. This can lead to innovative solutions that may not have been considered otherwise, resulting in better outcomes for everyone.

4 **Avoiding Stalemate:** Without compromise, conflicts can easily reach a stalemate where

neither side is willing to budge. This prolongs the dispute and can lead to negative consequences for all parties involved.

5 **Promoting Fairness:** Compromise allows for a fair distribution of benefits and concessions, ensuring that no one party is unfairly advantaged or disadvantaged. This fosters a sense of equity and justice in the resolution process.

6 **Building Trust:** Successfully reaching compromises builds trust and goodwill among parties, laying the groundwork for future cooperation and conflict resolution efforts.

7 **Minimizing Costs:** Conflicts can be costly in terms of time, resources, and emotional energy. Compromise helps to minimize

these costs by swiftly resolving disputes and allowing parties to move forward with their goals.

Finding Common Ground

Finding common ground is essential for effective communication and conflict resolution, especially when faced with seemingly irreconcilable disagreements. Here are some methods for exploring and achieving common ground with others:

1 **The "I" Statement Technique**: Express your perspective using "I" statements to avoid sounding accusatory. For example, say, "I feel that..." instead of "You always..."

2 **Acknowledge Valid Points**: Acknowledge the validity of the other person's concerns or points of view. This validates their

perspective and opens the door for reciprocity.

3 **Brainstorming and Problem-Solving Sessions**: Engage in collaborative problem-solving sessions where both parties can contribute ideas and potential solutions. Focus on generating creative options that address each party's interests.

4 **Use of Neutral Language**: Choose neutral and non-confrontational language to prevent the conversation from becoming emotionally charged. This helps in keeping the dialogue constructive.

5 **Building on Common Ground**: Identify and build upon the areas where agreement already exists. This can serve as a foundation for exploring solutions to more contentious issues.

6 **Break Down the Issue**: If the disagreement is multifaceted, break it down into smaller, more manageable components. Addressing one aspect at a time may make it easier to find common ground on specific points.

7 **Create a Safe Environment**: Foster an environment where both parties feel safe expressing their opinions without fear of judgment. This can encourage open communication and a willingness to explore common ground.

8 **Educate Each Other**: Take the time to educate each other about your perspectives, experiences, and concerns. Increased understanding can lead to empathy and the discovery of common ground.

9 **Use Visual Aids**: Sometimes, visual aids like charts, graphs, or diagrams can help clarify complex issues and facilitate mutual understanding.

10 **Time-Outs and Cooling-Off Periods**: If emotions are running high, consider taking a break and coming back to the discussion with a fresh perspective. A cooling-off period can prevent impulsive reactions and promote a more rational conversation.

11 **Trial and Error**: Be open to trying out different solutions on a trial basis. This approach allows for experimentation and adjustments, increasing the likelihood of finding a solution that works for both parties.

12 **Establish Clear Communication Norms**: Set ground rules for the conversation, such as

taking turns speaking, avoiding interruptions, and focusing on the issue at hand rather than personal attacks.

13 **Use Humor**: Appropriately injecting humor into the conversation can lighten the mood and create a more relaxed atmosphere, making it easier to find common ground.

14 **Seek Common Values and Goals**: Explore shared values and overarching goals that can serve as a common foundation for finding solutions.

Communication Skills

Clear and respectful communication is the cornerstone of healthy relationships, especially when navigating power dynamics. Here's why it's so crucial:

1 **Mutual Understanding:** Clear communication ensures that both parties understand each other's perspectives, needs, and boundaries. This understanding is essential for navigating power dynamics because it prevents misunderstandings and allows for fair negotiation.

2 **Respectful Dialogue:** Respectful communication fosters an environment where both individuals feel valued and heard. In relationships with power imbalances, respectful dialogue prevents the misuse of power and promotes equality.

3 **Conflict Resolution:** Power dynamics can often lead to conflict if not addressed properly. Clear communication provides a constructive way to resolve conflicts by encouraging open discussion, active listening, and compromise.

4 **Empowerment:** When communication is clear and respectful, it empowers both individuals to express themselves authentically and assert their needs. This empowerment is particularly important in relationships where one person may hold more power than the other.

5 **Building Trust:** Trust is the foundation of any healthy relationship. Clear and respectful communication builds trust by creating a safe space for vulnerability and honesty. This trust is essential for navigating

power dynamics, as it ensures that both individuals feel secure in their relationship.

Overall, clear and respectful communication is essential for navigating power dynamics within relationships because it promotes understanding, respect, conflict resolution, empowerment, and trust. By prioritizing communication, individuals can build healthier, more equitable relationships where power is shared and respected.

Effective Negotiation Strategies

Effective negotiation is a multifaceted skill that involves a combination of strategies and techniques. Here are some key approaches, including active listening, empathy, and understanding the other party's perspective:

1 **Active Listening**: This involves fully concentrating, understanding, responding, and then remembering what is being said. It's crucial to pay attention not only to the words but also to the emotions and body language of the other party.

By actively listening, you demonstrate respect and create an atmosphere of trust, which can lead to more open and productive discussions.

2 **Empathy**: Empathy is the ability to understand and share the feelings of another person. It's essential in negotiation because it allows you to connect with the other party on a human level, showing that you acknowledge their perspective and concerns. When both parties feel understood, it becomes easier to find

mutually beneficial solutions.

3 **Understanding the Other Party's Perspective**: Take the time to put yourself in the other party's shoes. Consider their motivations, interests, and constraints. Understanding their perspective helps you tailor your approach and proposals in a way that resonates with their needs and priorities. This can increase the likelihood of finding common ground and reaching a favorable outcome for both parties.

4 **Effective Communication**: Clear and concise communication is essential in negotiation. Be articulate about your own needs and interests while also being open to hearing the other party's viewpoints. Avoid making assumptions and seek clarification when necessary to ensure mutual understanding.

5 **Problem-Solving Mindset:** Approach negotiation as a collaborative problem-solving process rather than a win-lose scenario. Focus on finding creative solutions that address the interests of both parties and maximize value. Brainstorming together can lead to innovative ideas and compromises that wouldn't have been possible otherwise.

6 **Maintaining Flexibility:** Negotiation often involves give-and-take, so it's important to remain flexible and adaptable throughout the process. Be open to exploring different options and be willing to adjust your position if it helps move the discussion forward and achieve a mutually satisfactory agreement.

7 **Building Rapport and Trust**: Building a positive relationship with the other party can facilitate more productive negotiations. Find common ground, show appreciation for their perspective, and be genuine in your interactions. Trust is essential for effective collaboration and can help overcome potential barriers or conflicts.

8 **Preparation and Information Gathering**: Thorough preparation is key to successful negotiation. Research the relevant facts, figures, and background information beforehand. Understand your own goals and priorities as well as those of the other party. Having a well-informed perspective strengthens your position and enhances your credibility during the negotiation process.

Self-awareness and Emotional Intelligence

Developing self-awareness and emotional intelligence is crucial for effectively navigating the complex landscape of relationships.

It begins with introspection, where individuals delve deep into understanding their own thoughts, emotions, strengths, and limitations. By reflecting on past experiences and examining their reactions, they can identify patterns and triggers, gaining valuable insights into their behavioral tendencies.

This self-awareness serves as a foundation for emotional intelligence, which involves not only recognizing one's own emotions but also understanding and empathizing with the emotions of others.

Through active listening and genuine curiosity, individuals can tune into the feelings and perspectives of those around them, fostering deeper connections and mutual understanding.

Moreover, honing emotional intelligence equips individuals with the ability to regulate their own emotions, especially in high-stakes or challenging situations. By maintaining composure and making thoughtful, empathetic responses, they can navigate relationships with poise and resilience, even amidst conflict or adversity.

Furthermore, developing emotional intelligence involves continuously refining interpersonal skills such as communication, conflict resolution, and negotiation.

In essence, the journey towards self-awareness and emotional intelligence is ongoing, requiring dedication, introspection, and practice. Yet, the rewards are invaluable, empowering individuals to navigate relationships with authenticity, empathy, and integrity, ultimately fostering healthier and more collaborative environments.

Long-term Relationship Management

Whether in personal relationships or business partnerships, nurturing long-term connections requires dedication, empathy, and effective communication. Here are some strategies to consider:

1 **Open Communication:** Encourage transparent and open communication from

the outset. Create a safe space where both parties feel comfortable expressing their thoughts, concerns, and aspirations. Regular check-ins and honest conversations can prevent misunderstandings and build trust over time.

2 **Active Listening**: Practice active listening by paying full attention to the other person's words, thoughts, and feelings. This not only demonstrates respect but also helps in understanding their perspective deeply. Validate their experiences and emotions to strengthen the bond between you.

3 **Empathy and Understanding**: Cultivate empathy by putting yourself in the other person's shoes. Understand their needs, motivations, and challenges. Showing empathy fosters a sense of connection and

encourages cooperation, even during difficult times.

4 **Consistency and Reliability**: Be consistent and reliable in your actions and commitments. Consistency builds trust and reliability reassures the other person of your dedication to the relationship. Follow through on promises and obligations to maintain credibility.

5 **Adaptability and Flexibility**: Recognize that relationships evolve over time and be willing to adapt to changing circumstances. Flexibility allows for accommodating each other's growth, adjusting expectations, and finding mutually beneficial solutions to challenges.

6 **Conflict Resolution Skills**: Develop effective conflict resolution skills to address

disagreements constructively. Instead of avoiding conflicts, approach them as opportunities for growth and understanding. Focus on finding win-win solutions that honor both parties' needs and perspectives.

7 **Celebrate Successes and Milestones**: Acknowledge and celebrate achievements, milestones, and shared successes along the way. Celebrating together strengthens the bond and reinforces a sense of partnership and collaboration.

8 **Invest in Personal Growth**: Encourage personal growth and development for both parties. Support each other's goals and aspirations, whether professional or personal. By investing in each other's growth, you foster a sense of mutual

support and admiration.

9 **Respect Boundaries**: Respect each other's boundaries, preferences, and autonomy. Avoid imposing your own expectations or agendas onto the other person. Honor their individuality and autonomy while nurturing the connection you share.

10 **Regular Evaluation and Feedback:** Periodically evaluate the health of the relationship and solicit feedback from each other. Reflect on what's working well and areas that may need improvement. Use feedback as an opportunity for growth and refinement.

Chapter 10

Embracing Realistic Expectations

In relationships, it's crucial to have realistic expectations and to acknowledge that love, while beautiful and powerful, has its limits. Realistic expectations involve understanding that no relationship is perfect, and that love alone cannot solve all problems or fulfill every need.

Firstly, it's important to recognize that people are inherently flawed and imperfect. No one can be everything to someone else, and expecting perfection from your partner or from the relationship itself is setting yourself up for disappointment.

Understanding and accepting your partner's imperfections, as well as your own, is a key aspect of fostering a healthy and realistic relationship.

Additionally, it's vital to acknowledge that love does not automatically solve all conflicts or challenges that arise within a relationship. While love can provide support, comfort, and motivation to work through difficulties, it cannot magically erase differences or resolve deep-seated issues.

It's essential to communicate openly and honestly with your partner, to address problems as they arise, and to be willing to compromise and find solutions together.

Furthermore, it's important to have individual identities and pursuits outside of the relationship. Relying solely on your partner for fulfillment and happiness can place undue pressure on the relationship and ultimately lead to disappointment.

Maintaining a sense of independence and pursuing your own interests allows each partner to grow as individuals, which in turn enriches the relationship.

Ultimately, realistic expectations in relationships involve understanding that love is not a cure-all and that both partners are human, with their own strengths, weaknesses, and limitations.

By acknowledging these realities and approaching the relationship with honesty, empathy, and a willingness to work through challenges together, couples can build a strong foundation for a fulfilling and lasting partnership.

Managing Disappointment

Managing disappointment can be challenging, but there are several effective strategies to cope with it in healthy ways:

1 **Practice self-compassion:** Be kind to yourself when things don't go as planned. Acknowledge your feelings of disappointment without judgment. Remind yourself that it's natural to feel this way and that everyone experiences setbacks at some point.

2 **Seek support from loved ones:** Reach out to friends, family members, or mentors who can offer empathy, encouragement, and a listening ear. Talking about your feelings with someone you trust can help you process your emotions and gain

perspective.

3 **Reframe perspectives:** Try to reframe the situation by focusing on the positives or finding a silver lining. Instead of dwelling on what went wrong, look for lessons learned or opportunities for growth. Shifting your perspective can help you see the situation from a different angle and move forward with resilience.

4 **Practice gratitude:** Cultivate gratitude by focusing on the things in your life that you're thankful for, even in the face of disappointment. Keeping a gratitude journal or simply taking a moment each day to reflect on the good things in your life can help shift your mindset toward appreciation and positivity.

5 **Acceptance:** Accept that disappointment is a natural part of life and that not everything will go according to plan. Embrace the idea that setbacks and challenges are opportunities for learning and personal development. By accepting reality as it is, you can free yourself from unnecessary suffering and find peace in the present moment.

6 **Set realistic expectations:** Reflect on whether your expectations were realistic and adjust them if necessary. Sometimes, disappointment arises from setting overly high or unrealistic expectations. By setting more realistic goals and expectations, you can reduce the likelihood of disappointment in the future.

7 **Focus on what you can control:** Instead of dwelling on things beyond your control, focus your energy on the aspects of the situation that you can influence. Identify actionable steps you can take to improve the situation or work toward your goals, and take proactive measures to move forward.

Cultivating Realistic Expectations

Cultivating realistic expectations in relationships is crucial for fostering healthy and fulfilling connections. Here are some tips and techniques to help achieve this:

1 **Self-awareness:** Start by understanding your own needs, desires, and limitations. Recognize any unrealistic expectations you might have inherited from media, past

experiences, or societal norms.

2 **Communication**: Open and honest communication is key. Talk with your partner about your expectations and listen to theirs. Discuss what is feasible and what might be unrealistic. This dialogue can help manage each other's expectations effectively.

3 **Acceptance of imperfections**: Understand that no one is perfect, including yourself and your partner. Embrace each other's flaws and quirks as part of what makes you unique individuals.

Realize that imperfections are natural and can actually strengthen the bond between you.

4 **Letting go of fantasies**: Fantasies can sometimes set unrealistic standards for

relationships. While it's okay to have dreams and aspirations, it's important to distinguish between healthy aspirations and unattainable fantasies.

Focus on building a connection based on reality rather than chasing an idealized version of love.

5 **Flexibility and compromise**: Relationships require compromise and flexibility. Understand that you and your partner may have different perspectives, preferences, and needs.

Be willing to meet halfway and find solutions that work for both of you. This doesn't mean sacrificing your own happiness, but rather finding a balance that respects both individuals.

6 **Managing comparison:** Avoid comparing your relationship to others, especially those portrayed in the media or on social media. Remember that what you see on the surface may not reflect the reality of those relationships. Focus on your own journey and what works best for you and your partner.

7 **Gratitude and appreciation:** Cultivate a mindset of gratitude and appreciation for your partner and the relationship you share. Acknowledge the efforts and sacrifices made by both parties, and express your gratitude regularly. This can help foster a deeper connection and mitigate unrealistic expectations.

8 **Seeking support:** If you find it challenging to let go of unrealistic expectations or

embrace imperfections, consider seeking support from a therapist or counselor. Professional guidance can provide valuable insights and strategies for cultivating healthier relationship expectations.

Celebrating the Real

Let's embark on a journey to celebrate the raw, unfiltered beauty of real, imperfect love—a love that defies the glossy, airbrushed images often portrayed in movies and fairy tales.

Instead, let's revel in the messy, unpredictable, and profoundly human aspects of relationships that make them so uniquely special.

In a world where perfection is often held up as the ultimate goal, it's easy to overlook the richness found in the imperfections of love.

Real love isn't about flawless performances or scripted moments; it's about embracing the authenticity of our connections and cherishing them for all their quirks and complexities.

Picture the scene: two people, navigating the twists and turns of life together, each carrying their own baggage, dreams, and insecurities.

In this dance of souls, there are bound to be missteps, misunderstandings, and moments of doubt. But therein lies the beauty of it all—the messy, unpredictable journey of growth and discovery that love entails.

It's in the midst of disagreements, when tempers flare and egos clash, that we have the opportunity to truly see and understand one another.

It's in those vulnerable moments of conflict resolution that the bonds of trust and empathy are forged, paving the way for deeper intimacy and connection.

And what about the small, everyday gestures that often go unnoticed? The way one partner makes coffee just the way the other likes it, or the shared laughter over a silly joke that only the two of them understand.

These seemingly insignificant moments are the building blocks of intimacy—the threads that weave together the fabric of a life shared in love.

But perhaps most importantly, real love is about acceptance—acceptance of each other's flaws, quirks, and idiosyncrasies. It's about seeing beyond the surface to the essence of who we are and loving fiercely, unconditionally, and without reservation.

So let's raise a toast to the messy, imperfect, beautifully real love that fills our lives with meaning and purpose. Let's embrace the bumps in the road, knowing that they only serve to deepen our connection and strengthen our bond.

For in the end, it's not the picture-perfect moments that define us, but rather the messy, imperfect, wonderfully human journey of love that we share together.

Chapter 11

Finding Harmony in Imperfection

In the symphony of love and relationships, imperfections compose the most beautiful melodies.

It's crucial to understand that perfection is an illusion—a mirage that leads us down a path of frustration and disappointment. Instead, embracing imperfections is the cornerstone of genuine connection and lasting harmony.

In every individual, there exists a unique mix of flaws and virtues. It's these imperfections that make us human, relatable, and ultimately lovable. Striving for an unattainable ideal only serves to obscure the true beauty that lies within ourselves and our partners.

Acceptance is the key that unlocks the door to profound intimacy. When we accept our own imperfections, we cultivate self-compassion and authenticity. Similarly, when we embrace the imperfections of our partners, we foster empathy, understanding, and deep affection.

True love isn't found in flawless exteriors but in the messy, intricate landscapes of our hearts. It's in the moments of vulnerability, where imperfections are laid bare, that true connection flourishes.

In accepting imperfections, we pave the way for growth, forgiveness, and resilience within our relationships.

So, let's celebrate the quirks, the idiosyncrasies, and the imperfections that make us who we are. For it's in embracing the entirety of ourselves and our partners that we discover the true magic of love—a symphony of imperfection that resonates with the beauty of humanity.

Wisdom and Humility

Approaching relationships with wisdom and humility is akin to navigating life's most intricate dance.

It's about understanding that each of us carries limitations, biases, and imperfections that shape our interactions with others. By acknowledging these realities, we open ourselves to a journey of growth and discovery within our relationships.

Wisdom prompts us to reflect on our past experiences, to glean insights from both triumphs and tribulations. It teaches us to embrace the lessons learned from love's victories and defeats alike, understanding that each encounter offers a chance for personal evolution.

Moreover, wisdom encourages us to recognize the inherent complexity of human connection, reminding us to approach relationships with patience, empathy, and understanding.

Humility serves as a guiding light on this journey, reminding us of our own fallibility and the boundless depths of human emotion. It encourages us to set aside pride and ego, fostering an environment where vulnerability and authenticity can thrive.

Through humility, we come to appreciate the unique perspectives and experiences of our partners, fostering deeper connections built on mutual respect and admiration.

Together, wisdom and humility form the cornerstone of healthy, fulfilling relationships. They empower us to navigate the highs and lows of love with grace and resilience, fostering an environment where growth, understanding, and mutual support can flourish.

So, let us embrace these virtues as we embark on the beautiful, transformative journey of love.

Ebb and Flow of Human Connections

Human connections, in their essence, mirror the ever-changing tides of the sea—constantly shifting, sometimes calm and tranquil, other times turbulent and unpredictable.

Like a delicate dance between two souls, relationships embody a dynamic interplay of emotions, experiences, and shared moments.

Understanding and accepting the natural ebb and flow of these connections is fundamental to fostering healthy and enduring relationships.

Just as rivers carve their paths through landscapes, relationships evolve and adapt over time, shaping and reshaping the contours of our lives.

At the heart of this evolution lies the necessity for adaptability and patience from both partners.

Much like a garden requires nurturing and tending to flourish, relationships demand ongoing care and attention. This entails embracing change with an open heart and mind, recognizing that growth often arises from the challenges and trials encountered along the way.

In the tapestry of human connection, there are seasons of warmth and intimacy, where hearts beat in harmony and souls intertwine effortlessly. These are the moments when love feels like a gentle breeze, carrying us closer together in a symphony of shared dreams and aspirations.

Yet, amidst the serenity, there are also moments of discord and distance—inevitable phases where the currents of life pull us apart, testing the strength of our bond. It is during these times that patience becomes our guiding compass, anchoring us through the stormy seas of uncertainty and doubt.

True resilience in relationships emerges from the willingness to weather these storms together, hand in hand, trusting in the power of love to navigate us safely to calmer shores.

It requires a deep understanding that growth often occurs in the spaces between the notes, in the moments of tension and conflict that ultimately pave the way for deeper connection and understanding.

In essence, acknowledging the fluidity of human connections is an invitation to embrace the beauty of impermanence—to savor each moment shared, knowing that it is fleeting yet infinitely precious.

It is a testament to the richness of the human experience, reminding us that true love is not stagnant but rather a living, breathing entity that thrives on adaptability, patience, and unwavering commitment.

Conclusion

As we reach the culmination of our journey through the intricacies of human relationships, we are reminded of the profound truth that lies at the heart of our exploration: imperfection is the very essence of our humanity, and it is within this imperfection that we find the potential for true connection and harmony.

In "Harmonizing Imperfections: Finding Balance and Respect in Relationships," we have traversed the landscapes of love, vulnerability, power dynamics, accountability, and wisdom.

We have delved deep into the complexities of human connection, confronting the challenges and embracing the beauty found within the imperfect tapestry of our relationships.

Through our exploration, we have discovered that true respect and balance in relationships require a delicate dance—a dance that honors the autonomy and dignity of each individual while fostering a deep sense of empathy, understanding, and compassion.

We have learned that accountability is not a burden to be avoided but a pathway to growth and healing, and that wisdom is cultivated through experience, reflection, and an open heart.

As we bid farewell to these pages, let us carry forward the lessons learned and the insights gained into our own lives and relationships.

Let us strive to embrace the imperfections that make us human, to navigate the complexities of connection with grace and intention, and to cultivate relationships that are built on a foundation of mutual respect, understanding, and love.

May we continue to seek harmony in the midst of imperfection, knowing that it is through our shared humanity that we find our greatest strength and our deepest connections.

And may our journey toward harmonizing imperfections be a lifelong pursuit—one filled with growth, discovery, and the enduring beauty of genuine connection.